Fingerlings™

friendship @ your fingertips

Meet the
Fingerlings

Rosie Peet

Editor Rosie Peet
Senior Designer Lisa Robb
Pre-Production Producer Kavita Varma
Producer Louise Daly
Managing Editor Paula Regan
Design Manager Jo Connor
Publisher Julie Ferris
Art Director Lisa Lanzarini
Publishing Director Simon Beecroft

Reading Consultant Linda B. Gambrell, Ph.D.

First American Edition, 2018
Published in the United States by DK Publishing
345 Hudson Street, New York, New York 10014

Page design copyright © 2018 Dorling Kindersley Limited
DK, a Division of Penguin Random House LLC

18 19 20 21 22 10 9 8 7 6 5 4 3 2 1
001–313668–Aug/2018

A catalog record for this book is available from the Library of Congress.

ISBN (Paperback): 978-1-4654-8268-6
ISBN (Hardback): 978-1-4654-8277-8

DK books are available at special discounts when purchased in bulk for sales promotions, premiums,
fund-raising, or educational use. For details, contact: DK Publishing SpecialMarkets, 345 Hudson Street,
New York, New York 10014
SpecialSales@dk.com

Printed and bound in the USA

www.dk.com
www.fingerlings.com

A WORLD OF IDEAS:
SEE ALL THERE IS TO KNOW

Contents

Meet the Fingerlings

These cute animals are called the Fingerlings.

They live in Melody Village.

Let's meet some of them!

Bella

This monkey is named Bella. She lives in the treetops with her friends.
She loves jumping and climbing!

Boris

Boris is Bella's twin brother.

He has lots of energy.

He likes rock music.

He plays the drums loudly!

Finn

Mia

10

Hanging out

Bella and Boris have lots of monkey friends to play with.

Sophie

Zoe

Gigi

Meet Gigi the unicorn.
She loves parties with
her friends.
Gigi spreads fun wherever
she goes!

Sweet dreams

Gigi is dreaming of all her favorite things.

Glitter

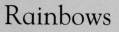

Rainbows

Candy

Fluffy clouds

Taking
selfies

Marge

Marge is a sloth.
She is very smart.
She likes reading books.
She also likes exploring
new places.

Kingsley

Kingsley is Marge's brother.
He is a chilled-out sloth.
He likes to relax.
His favorite hobby is surfing.

19

Party time

The Fingerlings love to play together.

When they play together,
the fun never stops!

Quiz

1. Where do the Fingerlings live?

2. What musical instrument does Boris play?

3. Which Fingerling loves to read?

4. Who likes surfing?

5. What kind of animal is Gigi?

Index

Quiz Answers

1. Melody Village, 2. Drums, 3. Marge, 4. Kingsley, 5. A unicorn

A LEVEL FOR EVERY READER

This book is a part of an exciting four-level reading series to support children in developing the habit of reading widely for both pleasure and information. Each book is designed to develop a child's reading skills, fluency, grammar awareness, and comprehension in order to build confidence and enjoyment when reading.

Ready for a Level 1 (Learning to Read) book

A child should:

- be familiar with most letters and sounds.
- understand how to blend sounds together to make words.
- have an awareness of syllables and rhyming sounds.

A valuable and shared reading experience

For many children, learning to read requires much effort, but adult participation can make reading both fun and easier. Here are a few tips on how to use this book with an early reader:

Check out the contents together:

- tell the child the book title and talk about what the book might be about.
- read about the book on the back cover and talk about the contents page to help heighten interest and expectation.
- chat about the pictures on each page.
- discuss new or difficult words.

Support the reader:

- give the book to the young reader to turn the pages.
- if the book seems too hard, support the child by sharing the reading task.

Talk at the end of each page:

- ask questions about the text and the meaning of the words used—this helps develop comprehension skills.
- read the quiz at the end of the book and encourage the reader to answer the questions, if necessary, by turning back to the relevant pages to find the answers.

Series consultant, Dr. Linda Gambrell, Distinguished Professor of Education at Clemson University, has served as President of the National Reading Conference, the College Reading Association, and the International Reading Association.